Mammoth Melting Sugar

(poems seasoned and simmered
in vegetables from the heart)

Rayfer E. Mainor, poet laureate
with Sarah "SJ" Mainor

A Royal *INK* Book
Published by 484 Publishing Group
Dallas, TX

Copyright © 2010 by Sarah "SJ" Mainor

ISBN: **978-0615501857**

Book Cover Design by Cicely's Jazzy Art

All rights reserved. No part(s) of this book may be reproduced, photographed, or printed through any form without prior written permission from the publisher.

Send inquiries to: info@remfoundation.org

484 Publishing Group Edition: October 2010
Manufactured in the United States of America

Poet Laureate Rayfer E. Mainor: *In Profile*
(March 25 1948-April 26 2008)

Award-winning poet/writer Rayfer E. Mainor began writing poetry at just 7 years old. Like many young writers, *poetry writing* was an outlet for Mainor to express his thoughts in a creative and constructive way. As a young adult, he discovered his true passions were not only molded into writing about human experiences but about taking action and advocating to see a positive change.

During his tenure that spawned over 50 years; Rayfer Mainor worked diligently as a Poet, Teacher, Entertainment Journalist and Professional Mental Health Counselor.

In this special book of poetry, "Mammoth Melting Sugar", Mainor stirs up a hefty spoonful of Knowledge, Encouragement, Love and Hope for all mankind but especially for the oppressed and misguided youth's soul.

"Mammoth Melting Sugar" is Mainor's 4th published book of poetry.

For my nephew

"Teddy P"

Contents
Mammoth Melting Sugar

Poet in Profile 4
Dedication 5

7th heaven 10
You must eat 13
Peas in a "Universal" Pod 14
Collards 15
Irish Papas 16
Curls, Naps & Oreos 17

Youngin' 18
Taboo 19
Noggins and Beans 20
Jellybeans and Gumdrops 21
African Violets…and Black- eyed Susans' 22
"Buds"…can wait 23
"The Killing of the Butterfly"… For Emmit 24

Arrested 26
Dead From the Neck Up 27
Fireflies, Lightning bugs and Glowworms 29
Don't let it bother you 30
Hopes and Regrets all day 31
When killing boys for fun 32
Don't Feed the Gorillas 33
The Violence of Colors 35

From Brussels (my first reaction) 36
Rappin' 4 old school 39
Read 41
Thinking Cap 42
On the day of Pentecost 43
Devil B4 Midnight 44
Food 4 Thought 45
Stay poised 46
the little boy that would 47
I Learned My Lessons Well 48
Up Above the Moon 49
Expression*less* 50

In My Father's House 51
You Must be Born Again 52
Hopelessness 53
Golden apples. Stop, Watch, and Listen 54
ambiguous bump in the day 55
Priorities 56
Good together 57
As, 58
After Our Own Image 59

The Key 60
LIFE 61
…and so 63
The Way 65

Anthology 67
Acknowledgements 68

7th Heaven

Just gimme some
Slowed down,
Laid back music by
Marvin or Luther.
The eloquence of
Martin Luther, King Tut
And all his gold.

Give me Queen Nefertiti
Swingin' on my right arm
And Queen Latifah on the left.

Let me feel
The miracle air,
A drop of rain
And gentle wind.

Let me hear
Angelic sounds
Of Sparrows signing
And Children playing.
While I daydream
Of better days
And peaceful nights.

I'm tasting warm baked bread
Dipped in Honey molasses
Eyes cured with no contacts
Nor sun- framed glasses.

I'm reading all the while
Writing 'till sun down
And reciting my poetry
All over Paradise Town.

You Must Eat

Like The Tomatoes in Belgium
you are always growing.
(which is good)
But you a long ways....
From "Mission Accomplished."

You haven't ate
all of your vegetables yet.
You haven't been
around the real block.

I want you to ripe into old age
And see your leaves
turn into yellow.
But first----
You must travel
over the vast landscapes
of human experiences.

To reach and come to full season,
Water finds its own level.
You must find
a workable
meaning for life.

You must chart your way
through this unfamiliar
terrain called "The Universe".

May you pollinate
And vegetate and thrive
May you grow gutsy,
Strong -willed and wise.

With a heart of oak
And a head unbowed.

Peas in a "Universal" Pod

You're fresh
And you're green
Blessed by God,
But hardly seen.

Such a deciduous plant
Defying compilations
That says it can't.

But with Self-fertilization
And pollination
Hard work breeds cultivation.
Beneath the baby's breath
All that is worth having is
Worth waiting.

Be true to yourself,
Your family
And to the one
Whom created you first.

Before you knew you,
When you were
Just an imagination
He was there,
Planting and plowing
All of us,
Into a wonderful creation.

Collards

Up from Southern roots
smooth and abundant,
with love
with untrammeled
fury and ease.

You give me strength
to endure my tasks,
between bites and graces
and goodness of the heart.

You fill me
with food of fuel
and sustenance.

You spoon me
with balance
and fortification.

You give me
cause to gaze
at a silent moon;
smile with the stars
and feel the
warmness of the sun.

Irish Papas

half -cooked , half -baked
Yes...perhaps,
he's *almost* a man.

Unriped,
Yet, you up early
Stirrin' up
Bright and early
With the birds and the bees.

And word is-----
My Brotha comes too quick
On the draw.

Don't know why or what he sees
Don't know where his morality be.
Stop the rush, the impulse
The haste and the madness,
What's the hurry?
A new corner that will lead to
Empty gladness?

I do love ya,
And I really do care
But son *you* young,
You got time to spare.

Young Irish Papa
In soon enough time
And at just the right time
You'll be right there.

Curls, Naps
And Oreos

With hair that can't
Be parted with fingers
He was boyishly handsome.

Ultra hip, yet innocent
With enormous
wondering eyes.

And a face
both black
and white.

Brown he was
And what some
would often call
"Oreo."

However,
He had never
known the big
difference.

Youngin'

Say Youngin'
Had you been young
When I was,
Thangs still be about the same
Aint that much,
That've honestly changed.

There are still The Rules
And The Law,
Law*less* men
And their games
Politik'n with deceit and
Troublin' the oppressed
And dispossessed.

There are the Powers That Be
The Rule of The Might
New World Orders
And dem White Folks?

Still White.

Taboo?

I've foreglimpsed and saw
The unchartered sketches in
"The Writings on The Wall".

The forbidden and denial,
Beyond the pale of off limit places
You are walking on
Forbidden ground
Eating forbidden fruit
That says "no man's land my son."

There are the "thou-shall- knots"
The "don't do's"
And the "say no too's. "

And then there will
Come a time
When you will want to
Drop that coup,
And get on cue
And proceed
To get the real clue

Which turns out to be
All about you.

Noggins and Beans

After cold frost
I lay in warm soil
Harvesting the moon,
Kickin it with my cronies
Home boys and home girls, too.

I Jazzed June with
Black and White beans,
Brown Pinto beans
Kidney's fat, limas
And little Navy's small.

But we are all one
Living out loud
And dancing tall.

Why even the skinny string bean
Got some conversation today.

Ah Woe is me-
Now I've done spilled the beans
All over myself.

Jellybeans and Gumdrops

Let me tell you
something sincere,
speak of secrets
difficulties,
losses and fears.

I danced on slightly
crusted grounds-
stomped my way
through Johnson Grass and Cockleburs
reaching morning glories and nut sedges,

Those weeds didn't offend me.

Still I fought,
fighting Cutworms,
and Beetles and Maggots.
trying to reach the
tassels and the silk,
and the sweet confections of
Jelly beans and Gumdrops.

All of them,
too sweet
for my taste
but still I ate
too much and too soon
for my own good.

**African violet's
....and black- eyed Susan's**

did all the tilling
...once upon a time
the weeding, hoeing,
and pruning and planting.

one thing we clearly know
we should reap all that we are willing to sow
do all that it takes
to germinate and grow.

**We work the soil
We know the seasons
We cool the climate,
For Springtime and reason.**

Buds... Can Wait

And they will, Lord willing

They'll wait to blossom into bloom
Take root shoot forth and sprout wings

Emmit Till-"The Killing of The Butterfly"

His little heart quivers heavily beating,
There's gaspin, and fallin.

A shortness of breath.

By now,
His stomach muscles tighten
And real terror sits in
His constipated bowels.

With agony in his stomach,
He feels his belly eating itself
Paralyzed as he stares
And rides with them-
Down that dark dusty road
Deep, deep
Into the night's
Mysterious air.

He soon disappears
Deep into the darkness,
Thin stiff air.

They commit the heinous crime,
The horrifying senseless sin
He vanished from this earth.

And even still,
To this very day-
Whenever I think about it,

I go
Into my room;
Shut the door,
And I scream
And I sigh,
And shed tears
Of sorrow
For the young
And for the innocent
Butterfly.

Arrested

You say
You aint' tryin
To crimp and cramp
My style,
Jam me up
And block me out.

But you
Hinder me, hamper me
And hold me up.

With bricks and stones
You fence me in
And wall my gate.

You put up road blocks on my path
And backstops where I've been.

You encircle me
With Bamboo curtains
And put up milestones
Around my neck.

You put shackles of
Balls and chains
Around my feet
So that you may tell
Tall tells

Work your Black Magic
Tape my mouth shut
Tie up my hands and
Trudge my name in
Jet Black Sand.

You and you're bitter,
twisted lies.

You may disown my blood
But you can't
control my mind.

Dead From the Neck Up

The others still dance too,
With heads filled up
With feathers and air
Primal stupidity
And Reason less ness
In perceptiveness,
It is the blind
Leading the blind
With their myopic
dim- sighted visions
Blurred and blunt,
Dim and dumb

And boy, I'd tell ya
If I could say,
"Stay away from *them*",
I would.
They are not "right in the head."
Their disoriented behavior
Is so infectious,
They will form a chorus
Singing jingle bells,
When it is not yet
Christmas time
Belting all on one
ditzy, dangerous accord.

Fireflies, Lightning Bugs, and Glow Worms

My single desire is for you to lay
Lie in abatement and mollification
Lay in the flattering unction of your soul.

Lay without making out,
Spawning, performing acts
You won't be able to feed.

I want you
To be able to
Lie down when you lay,
Be at rest and able to sleep
Throughout the night
And for all good reasons.

I want you to be able to
Wake up in the morning,
Not looking back.

Not facing jail time, shooting up,
But simply stretching out.

And reaching toward the light
Expand , widen and broaden
And become larger.

Increase and flourish
Flame out, fan and flare
Like wild fires
Behind the Santa Ana winds.

Don't let it Bother You

Like some cabs
Who flee all Ninjas,
In some far and remote places
Like in New York and Yazoo.

Round midnight
Armed with myself,
Bewilderment stares from my eyes
Beyond the light,
And from the street lamps.

As long as I can walk,
I can move.

Swiftly and subtly-
Feel my pride,
As my scrotum taps.

I felt my sack and keys
I am not wavered
It doesn't bother me.

I look straight ahead
Down the long dark streets---
And press forward.

Hopes and Regrets all Day

Too many lost hopes
And broken promises
He went to bed early
Just to dream.

He had so many things
To dream about.

He awoke at four o'clock
Every Tuesday morning
Looking for consolation.

Feeling violently ashamed,
He left his room
So ferociously------

He forgot
To make up
The bed.

When Killing Boys
For Fun

From way far away
past abandon country roads;
Through the hot summer air
I still hear 'em pickin' cotton
In the fields.

I still hear them hanging from trees,
The air smells of ropes burnin'
Necks snappin'
White folks clappin'.

The small of my back
Wet with terror;
My body shivers,
And drips
Like running water.

Don't Feed the Gorillas

They want to deal off the bottom
And skim off the top
Who's hustling who?

They want to rope off,
Beat and root you on
Stick, sting and burn
Only to leave you
All alone.

By all means,
Don't feed the gorillas.

Don't take their wooden nickels
Don't let them sell you no golden bricks.

They are all shifty and tricky
And can be as slippery as eels.

Don't be led by the gyp joints,
Nor be led to the boiler room
Only to be left in the lurch
For this here, 'aint the holy church.

You must be told
That all that has glitter
Isn't gold.

They'd love to tell you otherwise----
'Dem crafty little willies!

Don't let them hypnotize ,
Mesmerize and plagiarize
Your hard earned work.

They are wolves in sheep's clothing
Asses in lion's skin.
They are only summer soldiers
They are like Brutus and Judas
And Iscariot kin.

Betta WATCH OUT... for that middle man
Please be aware
Of his silly songs
And dance.

Beware of those fast deals
Fast cars
And fast girls.

Fast guys with fast schemes
Stagnant goals with wistful dreams.

Beware of the hocus pocus
And the hanky panky too-
The mumbo
The jumbo
The smoke
In the mirrors.

For it is all
monkey business.

The Violence of Colors

Dressed in all red
And some adorned in blue feathers
These peacocks have grown so beautifully,
But they have not grown together.

They strut on solid ground
For they are too afraid to fly.

They rather
Battle the battle
Bruise each other
With sticks, whips,
Pistols and knives.

No new era
No true representation
No glory on the horizon
No true colors
Of our skin folk.

Please bothers, sisters
Fathers and mothers
Do all that you can to-----

STOP THE VIOLENCE.

From Brussels to Waco…
(my first reaction)

If Brussel Sprouts
Grow in Belgium
How they get to Waco, Texas?

What are they doing in my hood---
Growin' in my back yard?

They on my street,
And at my house
They on my table,
And on my plate
And what do ya mean…
I hafta eat them anyhow?

I was young back then.
I was "almost a man."

Today I know.
And wished I had,
Or could've walked
The Boulevards of Brabant.

Picking out the Sprouts myself
Near Brussel's open market places.

Teaming and throbbing
With activity
While gazing upon
The magnificence
And grand places.

To share my poems
With those inner city children
And to read their poetry in French.
To sit along the Sienna River
And climb the hills of Lautenberg
And wine and dine in sweet cuisine.

Read libraries filled with medieval
Central Africa and the Congo Museum
I'd stroll through Bois de La Cambria
I'd run across canals and through
Railroad stations, but take my time
In the botanical gardens
And quaint shops.
Stop to smell the tulips and daffodils
And feel on magic carpets and laces.
As I puff on their too expensive cigars.

I would drink their brew
And discuss the" Imitation of Life"
All the night long.

I'd feel at home,
With Symphony, Orchestra,
Ballet, Theater and Art.

I would dance a dance with Constantine
Learn them to sing, twist and shout.
Teach them how to do the "Shot Gun"
And be their last patriotic
Broke Rebellion out.

Rappin' for Old School

They sing about
What many of us
Sung for.

And since,
Many of us
Didn't get what
We sang for...

These young rappers,
Are singing about it
 With words glistened in anger
And in hopelessness too.

Interwoven and fashioned,
Into a faster beat
Impatiently they beat
And box.

And while some still sleep
They address the
Unaddressed.

In plain language
They rap fresh.

Consequently,
Unconstraint

And in anguish
Made real.
They rap raw,
With new energies
That everyone can feel.

They rap wild
And they rap hard.

With new attitude
Often misconstrued
As something less than
Art of a rebellion

They can rap.

In black macho and myth-
Mystically, mysteriously,
Blatant and Blunt---

They rap about every black
Conceivable emotion
Of yesterday
And of today.

Read

Finding anguish in "Invisible Men"
I, almost a man
Withdrew into a weary flight.
Receding into
More abstractions,
I exhausted myself
With Baldwin,
Malcolm and Dubois.

Thinking Cap

Come into the spirit of the age
And place your mind
Upon lofty thoughts.

And dream big.

Be a lover of wisdom,
Spirituality and intellect.

Leave the Knuckleheads
And Appleheads alone.

Venture off
Seek out
Socrates, Solomon
Buddah , Gandhi
Einstein, MLK,
And perhaps REM.

Search for their wise,
Sensible and prudent ideology.

With genuine open-mindedness
And a willingness to understand.

On the Day of Pentecost

My spirit intense
I did not speak
In unknown tongues.

Nor did I tarry
For very long.

I looked for Elijah and Abraham---
But they were not there.

Where have they all gone?

Devil fo' midnight

The evening sun was going down
And night had fallin'
"I think I'm coming to the end of my day now",
I concluded.

I've worked hard.
I've toiled.
I've labored.

I smiled at old Satan
Just sittin over there,
In old dirty work clothes----
In *my* easy chair.

Sippin' something' stale
Merciless and unchanging,
Smelling as real as the odor of death
Black eyes fixed on defeat and destruction.

Pursing his lips, giving me the evil glare
Figuring out…just how
He gone fool the Lord this time?

He then hid his face
As night continued
To fall.

Food for Thought

Apply yourself like car wax,
Zero in on life
And all the workings
Of the mind.

Stay focused using
Straight forward thinking
And common sense reasoning.

In whatever you do,
Think those things through
Take time to muse over it.

And when it is time
Ripe!
Ripe!
Ripe.

Enjoy the fruits
Of your labor.

Stay poised

To leap into the sky

Beat your wings

And dance up

With the wind

The Little boy that Would
-For all of the future Baracks,
and Poet Laureates

He was not to be doubted
It was self-evident, because he was sure.
He was sure as God made little green
Apples and little black boys
And sun-yellowed dandelions
He was sure.

He talked doubtlessly
And he questioned less,
He confirmed in his resolve.

Amazingly he was only,
A lad of seven years old
But with stability
And firmness in his mind,
He secured his thoughts.

He was filled with self-confidence
And with poise and self-assurance
And courage,
He unafraid
And without batting and eye
MOVED.

His moves were unmistakable moves
They were with absolute certainty,
And surefire determination.

I learned my Lessons Well

I too, once was green.

I was gullible, and seducible
Too soft, too weak
And naïve.

I fell under charms
And spells and
Over trusting.

Beyond misbelieve and
The shadows of doubt
Beyond skeptics
And suspicions.

Up Above The Moon

>Beyond the night
>Far out of sight;
>Beyond its glow
>And visibility.
>
>Beyond air and sky
>And unanchored,
>communities of life.
>
>Far beyond my childhood dreams,
>Beyond the beats of my own heart.
>
>So far, so far away---
>But I kept thinking....
>
>L.A.
>
>is only a day's
>drive away.

Expressionless

When my voice returned to me
at about 18 o'clock in the am,
Still my mind could not grasp it
I wasn't even quite sure
What I loss or why I lost it.

But nevertheless
Still, I lost.

Invisible strings, lips sealed
But about to break in silence.

There is nothing left here to discover
Because time took it all away.

In My Father's House
There are many mansions

There is a better place,
In Bulah's hand
Where I can lay down
In the happy hunting
Grounds in Elysian fields.

I can rest in Abraham's bosom,
 sleep 'til kingdom come
And awake before
 The presence of
God.

You Must Be Born Again

For those who have
Walked the earth,
The living and the breathing
And the quick and the dead.

You must wake up
Be born again
Rise and resuscitate.

See the height,
And become new,
Once more again.

Have a tenacious
Love affair
With this thing
Called life.

Hopelessness

Smoky too many cigarettes
Smoky too many blunts
Left for days on in
Slowly beginning
To look like a runt.

Hell yes, Sirs' and Mams'
I've been working all these jobs.

Bustin' my tale
Seven days and no vacations.

So what on earth
Do I have to show
For it?
Still don't seem like
I've moved farther than an inch.

With nothin to show
For it.

golden apples. Stop. Watch. & Listen.

Listen to the inner hush
And the lucid stillness,
Don't be surprised
Fear not.

You can't afford to fear them,
LISTEN to what they are saying

And most of all...WATCH
 What they are doing.

Real Friends
are not defined by Silence
Or by how hard
They are or appear to be.
Real Friends
are defined by
What they say or do.

Their words,
Their character
And their deeds.

ambiguous bump...in the day

I knew there was something
Strange about today,
I don't know why I felt
Suddenly that something
Peculiar would come my way.

But all of a sudden
It hit me
Hit me
Hard.

I held my head in my hands
One hot windless day in May.
More treacherous than
The needed mist
All fighting for space.
I saw the blue sky tremble
As the sun melted the air.

It became unbearable to digest.
Surrounded by the brown landmass
Of dirt and cloud dust.
Gravity dipped back and forth
And I swore the earth shook.

Under my size 15
Square famed foot.

Priorities?

They Say,
"Stop worrying about
The Opponents and Foes".

They Say,
"Look out and become more concerned
About yourself and what's yours".

But I say,
"How far would we both really get"?

Brother Martin said that
"A Collective Conscious,
is what we really need".

Working hard to raise our families,
Building wealth, stopping violence
Confronting our enemies and imitators---

Priorities,
They are all ours.

Good Together

You're a person I find
A lot of peace in,
There's a calm in your eyes
And a love in your smile.

Plus, you crack me up
With laughter,
Leaving me in stitches.

Something marvelous happens
Each time I'm in your presence
Something seems to thunder in the air.

What a wonder you are
What a marvel you are
My brotha and My sista.

As

As touched as tomorrow
As children, not yet dreamed of ....
What may happen is far more important
Then what has happened.

After Our Own Image

We have sown the seeds
We must cultivate the soil
We must admonish the exhort
Endure and encourage
Advise and instruct.

For we are the forerunners,

We must pave the way
We must prepare them.

Train them
Teach them.

the key to the kingdom

                                                                you can't give up
                                                               you have much to do

                                      what is coming is already ready

                                                   there is so much more
                                                                    to come

LIFE

is exciting and effervescent
it tears with passion
and towers with rage
it can be intoxicating and inflammatory
violent and irascible
impassioned and mean.

it can be marvelous and amazing
wrapped in wonders
and surprise.

it can astound and astonish
and bewilder.

LIFE
is an awesome wonder.

it can enrapture, enravish,
and overwhelm you
don't be bewildered
or confound.

LIFE
is astonishing and impregnable
LIFE
is hard and tough and rugged.

you must be strong
have what it takes---the strength
of will to endure

to stand up, to bear up, to keep up
to hang in, hang tough, and to hold up,
to hold out, and hold on.

you must be invincible
unconquerable, unbeatable
unflagging and
unbowed.

Amen.

...and so,

I ask you to observe
And take caution.

Eat your vegetables,
Sons, and Daughters
Nephew and Nieces

Eat them Whole
Or eat them in pieces.

They will protect and insulate you
From the ravenous and voracious
Tapeworms that life dispenses.

From the cavities of naysayers that will
Burn with green envy from just the sight
Of you.

And they,
Those wholesome ones,
Loaded with
Vitamin A through Zinc----

Will help to protect
You from the
Irresolute coldness----
That this unpredictable
World will bring.

Somebody said:

"If you can conceive it , and believe it, you can achieve it"

In Love Story I wrote: "Faith is Power"
For Mammoth I write:

THE WAY

Put your stock and store
In faith, trust and hope
Believe without reservation.

Don't just knock on wood
And cross your fingers
But keep thinking and doing
Your absolute best.

Wake up! Look up!
Be wedded to
And certain of
The ending results
The final outcome.

Rest in confidence and
Have no misgivings
Put yourself in the hands
Of the hands that hold you,
Keep you, let you,
And enable you.

Stay of good cheer
And with high hopes
Enclosed in the silver lining

Have noble intentions.
And by all means,
Keep the Faith, baby.

Rock me in the cradle of love
Feed me till I want no more....

Anthology

Other books by Rayfer E. Mainor:

Poems-(1969)

Tribute to Blackness- (1975)

To Mister or Sarah Jean: A Love Story – (1985)

TRIBUTE: A *RE*Collection of poems by Rayfer E. Mainor – (TBA)

POET LAUREATE *"A Daughter's Memoir"* – (TBA)

Acknowledgements

Proverbs 3:3 *says:*
Let love and faithfulness never leave you; bind them around your neck, write them on the tablet of your heart. Then you will win favor and a good name in the sight of God and man.

I am forever indebted to the Lord above, for his blessings and unconditional Love. Thank you for guiding me through every step of this creative process.

A very special thanks to My dear Father ~Mr. Rayfer E. Mainor. You were the most loving father, the most giving friend, & one of the world's greatest literary talents! Without you, MMS, would not be possible. Your star is shining, your legacy is thriving. I love and miss you more each day~

Special thanks to our family, friends and lovers of poetry all over the world! Your support, encouragement and dedication are deeply appreciated.

SJM

Sarah "SJ" Mainor

Sarah "SJ". Mainor has taken audacious steps to follow in the huge footsteps of her beloved father Rayfer E. Mainor. SJ has participated with non-profit organizations in efforts to encourage, organize and work with community residents, particularly young adults in the southern zip codes of Dallas, TX, to forefront ongoing challenges, and develop influential power to promote and create change.

Mainor attest her father's wisdom and guidance as the inspiration for her forthcoming creative endeavors.

She is the Owner/Creative Director of 484 Publishing Group and currently resides in Dallas, TX

www.ingramcontent.com/pod-product-compliance
Lightning Source LLC
Chambersburg PA
CBHW051715040426
42446CB00008B/900